POEMSCAPES

AND *A LETTER TO GOD*

BY KENNETH PATCHEN

An Astonished Eye Looks Out Of The Air
A Surprise For The Bagpipe-Player
Before The Brave
Cloth Of The Tempest
Doubleheader
Fables & Other Little Tales
First Will & Testament
Glory Never Guesses
Hurrah For Anything
Memoirs Of A Shy Pornographer
Orchards, Thrones & Caravans
Panels For The Walls Of Heaven
Pictures Of Life And Of Death
Poemscapes
Poems Of Humor & Protest
Red Wine & Yellow Hair
See You In The Morning
Selected Poems
Sleepers Awake
The Collected Poems of Kenneth Patchen
The Dark Kingdom
The Famous Boating Party
The Journal Of Albion Moonlight
The Love Poems of Kenneth Patchen
The Teeth Of The Lion
They Keep Riding Down All The Time
To Say If You Love Someone
When We Were Here Together

KENNETH PATCHEN was born December 13, 1911, in Niles, Ohio, and educated at the Alexander Meiklejohn Experimental College of the University of Wisconsin. As a young man, he worked in a steel mill and held many other types of jobs, but after receiving a Guggenheim fellowship for a first book of verse, *Before the Brave* (1936), he has devoted himself to poetry, prose, and painting. Many of his works have been translated and published abroad; to date he has done more than 500 volumes in his "Painted Books" series.

In 1957 Patchen pioneered in the "public birth of Poetry-Jazz" by reading his poems to the accompaniment of the well-known Chamber Jazz Sextet in nightclubs and concert halls on the West Coast, breaking attendance records in San Francisco and Los Angeles. He went on to read successfully in the East and has also recorded his poetry under Cadence and Folkways labels.

Another Patchen innovation has been his "Picture Poems," first presented in book form in 1966 in New Directions' *Hallelujah Anyway*, though published earlier as a series of greeting cards. These are not illustrated poems but a new creative form, a true fusion of two arts. Working with watercolor, casein inks, and other media, Patchen blends word and image in intricate patterns of shape and meaning.

Patchen has lived in New York, Boston, Santa Fe, Phoenix, New Orleans, and Connecticut; he is married and currently resides on the California coast.

POEMSCAPES

Kenneth Patchen

AND *A LETTER TO GOD*

New Directions

FOR MIRIAM

POEMSCAPES

POEM I SCAPE

1) FASHIONED IN LOVE

Let it be fashioned in love! Boundless and imperturbable. Let it be!
O tiger sleeping in the rose-heart. Let it be! Masterless, remote,
solitary. A country where men and birds may come to take breath.

THAT COMES HERE! (2

I live in wonder. It is a glory to be alive in me. How there is
grief! How there is grief and joy! O how there is a grief and a joy
in me! The cursing prayer that is me! O far on the other side of me,
beyond senses' reach — *that* comes here!

3) LIFE IS PRAISE

O unto me be given praising's gift! Wonder and love! O wonder
and love!

AND GIVE BREATH (4

Beautiful are the trees, and the fields, and the waters. . . beautiful are the arms and throat of a woman. . . beautiful is the light
on this table here. . . beautiful there in the sky. . . *Life is only
beautiful.*

5) THE DANCING CHANCES

Throughout there is flowing. Statues, groves and stars. Nothing is still. All things are a returning. If we are to be all right, we must be getting ready to take something good back with us. Now.

CERTAINLY ENOUGH CUPS (6

The room is gay with cups. Thousands and thousands of them, big ones, little ones, clay, tin, china — there are even fifty of stone. The man who lives here is a cup, his wife is a cup. Their children are all cups except the oldest who is a saucer, and even he's cup-shaped.

7) ONE GRAY MORNING

"Dear friends" you are, at times, quite far away — after a manner of speaking.

FOG ROLLING IN (8

Old and forgotten they lie, ladies of all yesterday's evenings. Their noses and shanks bandaged with dirt; so. And with kings and sparrows. Today is June 18th. Nothing is ever stilled; in sorrow, in joy. . . *Flowing.*

POEM III SCAPE

9) THE LITTLE ESSAYS

Why Have Hands? They are, from time to time, useful. This has been, in many cases, established. They are mankind's only really trustworthy vocabulary, the nerves and muscles of the spirit made manifest. — Basically gay, unscientific.

MORE FABULOUS ANIMALS (10

This little fellow will delight you with his enthusiasm! He considers it a mark of special esteem to run up one's leg in search of spices which are an indispensable item of his fare. These he will find after arduous and oftentimes dangerous expeditions. One of a kind, his mating habits remain largely illusive.

11) GOLDEN PLUM BUDS

She loosens her hair. Out in the garden the flowers try on new colors.

MY JOURNEY'S JOURNEYING (12

Stand off! shouted the guard. Broken arrows bending up out of the silver quiver. . . He fired again and again across the harbor at us, the bullets glinting through the spongy tips like eyes in a bucket.

13) HOUSE OF TRIFLES

Pleasing and menacing, a house of trifles, and yet it must be possible to install a fountain somewhere. Sort of thing has been done, in the past at any rate. A fountain of rich, jetting blood.

THE LITTLE ESSAYS (14

Beethoven vs Statistics. Of course it requires little ingenuity to smell up quite a case against numbers. The case for them is likewise strong, however. What is the puzzled spectator to do? We know that Beethoven walked through parks with his hands in his pockets. This is the *practical* side to things: all else — minus a *plus*-ME.

15) THE BLIND WASHERWOMAN

Every evening she puts her pay into a flowered neckerchief and shuffles dustily drinkward.

GOLDEN PLUM BUDS (16

And now it is your grace that I would celebrate, O my flowering one. . . The roses walk upon the summer breeze never more lightly than thou upon these drab lanes of the village. . . Village? Nay! Paradise!

17) MORE FABULOUS ANIMALS

Nesting in threes, they waggle their long, skinny, yellow legs crazily about them. The females are usually very lazy, so nothing will do but somebody else lay their eggs. But in the nest, oh what jolly fun!

MY JOURNEY'S JOURNEYING (18

I am descended from a traveling people. Nothing would do but they go! They would travel any time of year, *anywhere*. "Let's go . . . Get going!" A kind of fermentation, a rash to the feet. But all I like about travel is getting out of places; the better the place the better I like scramming.

19) MY JOURNEY'S JOURNEYING

The yellow sponge of a streetlight in the rain. . . Gangrenous wounds of their cities. . .

MY INNOCENT COMPANIONS (20

This particular pair are constantly disappearing. One minute they're leaning out the window, laughing, calling something down to the postman; the next they've disappeared, leaving absolutely no trace. Once disappeared, they invariably, instantly, disappear again.

POEM VI SCAPE

21) THE TEMPLED LAMPS

The rain is falling. On the land, a disconcerting glitter of unimportantnesses — wagons, dogs, men. If it were not for the wide, chambered waters — so prudent, so renewingly clean — World, world, the lamps blurring out, out. . .

AN EXTRAORDINARY COMPLAINT (22

It is ruined, that admirable trade. Even the potato-appraiser can hold up his head on certain occasions, or hire somebody to do it for him. Not so with us. We are not shunned exactly, we are even much sought after in some circles; in fact, rather too much is made of us i s c.

23) THE VAST SHELTER

O the tiny red roofs there! the beautiful dynasty of flesh. . . Sing on, Heart!

ANOTHER DAY GONE (24

The sky is full of rain, a straining sack. A wet smell fills the house. I see that the light is thickening: on faces, an inch and a half; on things — carriages, trees — a good three-four inches.

25) THE LITTLE ESSAYS

Meaning of Objects. Liberty is not often thought of as an object, like a bruised apple for instance. But liberty is all-important; liberty is more all-important than anything. Hence liberty is the only *object*-object.

THE LITTLE ESSAYS (26

What is "Names"? Whenever this problem arises, it is necessary to maintain a nice perspective. For it is desirable to examine the thing carefully, possibly (even) get furiously involved in it. This business of "names" is killing the world, you know. Not all at one stroke, but miserably, snivelingly. Behind the masks, rot, corruption, hypocrisy.

27) MORE FABULOUS ANIMALS

When sunlight hits a green leaf just right, that makes him! Abundant in children.

MY INNOCENT COMPANIONS (28

Rarely discerned in marshy ground, they wear customarily great, elongated shoes which set them apart in any company. As though to compensate for this eccentricity of dress, they wear nothing else whatever. Magnificent sliders; leather-connoisseurs.

29) LOVE IS PLAYFUL

Love is playful, noble and ennobled, O shattering gentleness! the sober, sweet glee of its flowing wonder! O love is playful and undesigning! Ah, wrath of it, the wrath of a man's love seeking its channel!

THE WOODS MAIDEN (30

Early one evening I met the maiden of the wood. Leaves and stars like cold leaves were twined in her hair. Sorrow stood on her face as a music, and through her walking sounded the weeping of birds. Behind her, his horns raking the sky, strode a great black stag. In silence they passed.

31) SOMEWHERE IS FLEETING

"My" life — Out of the silence the first flakes of snow begin to fall. . .

THE HEART'S LANDSCAPE (32

In loving tenderness, whisper of flesh through the darkening curtain. . . Sorrow's music taking flight through these soft folds. . . In loving tenderness (and secret anguish), O intricate intentions, banners waving above invisible fortresses. . . Horizon of retreating silhouettes. . .

33) YOUNG GIRLS SWIMMING

Bodies like wavering, half-dissolving flowers, young girls swimming in the river. There! the pink, silken petal of a thigh! the clustering loveliness of a tiny breast! How very blue and pure the sky above them.

SOMETIMES IS NEVER (34

At the moment when the player for the highest stakes walks naked in the garden and there is no certainty for him and the tombs of youth echo only the decaying tramp of causes lost before attempted and the tigers on the shadowy riverbank cry piteously in their sleep and the chips prove counterfeit.

35) IN SUCH HARNESS

Out of the river rides a naked girl, shoulders of her horse star-lathered. . .

ONE SUMMER NIGHT (36

I formed a shawl of the water's shining, a clasp from a seabird's wing. . . for the skirt I took the mist from over a summer field. . . and with these I clothed her. . . her heart beating, *beating*. . .

POEM X SCAPE

37) GOLDEN PLUM BUDS

This night the wind moves almost without sound through the leaves of the tree beneath my window. I think of many things I would not willingly remember. The wind moves very quietly. The leaves hardly stir.

THE LITTLE ESSAYS (38

Wherefore & Henceforth. There is no disputing the miserable showing of the "average intelligence." Too often the inclination is rife to formulate principles along whose narrow highways some congress in "harmonious evaluations" may be precipitated, or at least partially *behaviorized*. This is palpable poppycock! Where does this leave INSTINCTIVE INSTINCT? Time somebody thought of that!

39) AT THIS MOMENT

As I say this a flashing wheel of children spins across the sun-drenched lawn!

A NIGHT SONG (40

When did my letter reach you? Had you already found the room you longed so hard for, or were (are) you still looking? I told you something in the letter I didn't mean to. — No matter.

41) AID TO DELIVERANCES

As an aid to deliverances, though by nature grave and troubled,
the Guardian of the Wall, whose own deepest, purest wish. . .
alas, alas, alas. . . by a terrible excess of gaiety *he will love and
help you.*

KINDNESS OF CLOWNS (42

The clowns have built a house in the forest, by sheer jest of
numbers. Then they want to move a clown from an alien league
into it. Until that moment no one had ever shown that clown any
kindness, so naturally he was suspicious. His father said those
fellows plan to steal your pants.

43) KINDNESS OF CLOWNS

(The father cannot be blamed for his suspicions. Bad blood
existed between the leagues.)

KINDNESS OF CLOWNS (44

But father's and son's suspicions were unfounded. The forest-
living clowns moved their rival into the house and fed him deli-
cious foods and let him win all the card games. This treatment
made him more suspicious.

45) NOT CHERISHED ENOUGH

I do not feel that it is cherished enough, this hesitant thing, shy under the fingers' touch. Planted in almost any soil, it would thrive, grow raptly sunward. More courageous than a lioness; more beautiful, too.

MY INNOCENT COMPANIONS (46

They are tirelessly searching for large bodies of dry water. In apartment houses, grain storagetanks, garages in the suburbs, literally anywhere, look closely and you are bound to spy them, their arms waving like antennas, noses stretched with sniffing, keen on the scent, positively enraptured! And what's more, they always *do* find them!

47) GETTING UP EARLY

Such a marvelous delicacy of castles shimmering out upon these bushes in the morninglight. . .

WHEN THAT HAPPENS (48

At no other call! Cherished at its *real* level! How joyous! How truly joyous! Even the touch of the fingers turning into curious plants that drink thirstily of the sun! Every nerve strumming like a wing!

49) THE FLUID APPEARANCES

Faithful to what enchants me. . . The rosy, singing fire of the living flesh! how splendid! O how splendid! what dazzling consolations! temptations! such durable halos! Today I'm lost in a mingling of fluid appearances. . . imperishable audacities. . . !

GOLDEN PLUM BUDS (50

Since it is as beautiful as it is, there will be nothing done in vain in this world. When it lay across my hand, the ardent glow of noon upon it, reverently, barely touching it, as a golden mouth lightly touches a forehead fashioned of cobwebs, I seemed to have entered an unsuspected portal.

51) SURROUNDED WITH ENCHANTMENTS

In the caress of shapes, colors, immaculate appearances. . . O we are surrounded with enchantments!

ABOUT MAKING JUDGMENTS (52

Well, I have not reserved judgment, that would be a terrible nuisance, my spirit could never stand it. I have, instead, made judgments about an astonishing number of matters. At their head: Who can judge anything?

53) THE PICKLED CHAFFINCH

Destiny unmakes strange bedfellows. There was once a great number of people hastening to an inn. "Plenty rooms" they kept saying. Actually there were only three. Moreover, the inn was closed for seasonal repairs and refurbishments.

THE LITTLE ESSAYS (54

Is Destiny Desirable? Fortunately an answer to this question will depend entirely on each individual's own presentiment. Some will endeavor to sidestep; others to deck themselves out in vague discretions, alluding perhaps to example, foreign to any normal experience. Nobody can really blame either faction: destiny, let's face it, is either desirable — or it is *undesirable*.

55) WHAT DESTINY DESIRES

Destiny is the music of the improbable. Were it otherwise, almost anyone could exist.

KINDNESS OF CLOWNS (56

Destiny made a shambles of their playful house in the forest. In the guise of a cyclone, followed by a violent explosion. The clowns and their reluctant guest (him of the rival league) scattered without further ado.

57) MY INNOCENT COMPANIONS

Perpetually leaping up and refusing to recognize chairmen. (As you know we have meetings here right along, every few minutes practically. Sometimes within a meeting there'll be a dozen other meetings. — "Who's that bum!" — "*Sit down!*"

MY JOURNEY'S JOURNEYING (58

Suppered at the inn. Nervous with those thousands of massive candles which walk lumberingly about between the tables, squirting a foul-smelling stuff out of their ears and guffawing uproariously each time the innkeeper drops a plate or a diner, braver than his fellows, openly expresses resentment at one of their unusually crass overtures.

59) WHAT STARTS WELL

They began by discussing the charming shoulders of bottles; ended seated on their own.

FRIEND THE RABBIT (60

Once outside the door we chanced to meet a rabbit on muleback going from house to house trying to sell shares in an unbigening block of ice. Mopping our brows, we wished him all the best.

61) KINDNESS OF CLOWNS

No sooner had the clowns got a new house built, a worse wind than the first blew it down. And it also re-blew down the old house which they had scarcely begun to prop up.

FRIEND THE RABBIT (62

The special, brilliant, ebullient way he rode astride his mule was a warming thing to see. One would surely credit him with enterprises of a most gleaming order. But it was precisely here that many experienced really annoying misgivings: (for all did wish him well — no wonder!) But he *did* do rather. . . odd things.

63) ON, ON, ON

Tremendous trifles — *On, on, on* — and then? Whitepanther beside the milk pitcher — Trifling tremendousnesses —

A NIGHT SONG (64

It has been a long time getting here, your letter. The leaves are nearly gone from the trees now. Saw something today in a shop-window which I wanted very badly to buy for you. — No matter.

65) THE FARAWAY BALLAD

Bloodred are the fishes that sleep in the grove. Bloodred are their dreaming faces, bloodred the leaflike scale on their little hands. Soon will the maidens come to wake them, the lilylike maidens. . .

THE FARAWAY BALLAD (66

Milkwhite are the fishes that sleep in the grove. Milkwhite the dreamlike glow from their little breasts that are so cold. Soon will the masters come to wake them, the masters of the longlost. . . O soon will the masters come in their snow-sheeted robes. . .

67) THE FARAWAY BALLAD

Deathcolored are the fishes that sleep in the grove. Deathcolored the fishes. . .

THE FARAWAY BALLAD (68

O the color of life itself are the fishes that sleep in the grove! Lifecolored are their slowly opening eyes, lifecolored the twiglike unfolding of their gentle hands! Soon they will come among us.

69) A NIGHT SONG

Each step down the lane to the mailbox is a kind of hell. There in the morning. . . *the sun. . . the birds singing all around me. . . everything green and clean-looking. . .* No letter from you. — From anyone.

FRIEND THE RABBIT (70

I like to think of him as he looked in his new suit of orange and white checks and pink velvet lapels. Hurrying along, whistling cheerfully, his mule having a smart time keeping pace. A gigantic sunflower behind either ear, a flaming red hat perched well back on his head. Hawking select unburial plots.

71) A NIGHT SONG

You once asked me what I wanted out of life. . . Let's say — No matter.

FRIEND THE RABBIT (72

They were both frowning up at the Tower Room, where sometimes lovely maidens have a hard deal escaping the clutches of wicked (but rich) kings. He whispered something to his mule, and — bam! ! ! no castle.

73) CONVERSATION WITH MIRRORS

"I don't always come off. . . umm, even second best." — "But you do have a fancy of yourself walking? I mean, when you *are* walking, not just sitting, or, perhaps, even, well, reclining." — "You didn't mention *running*. . ."

CONVERSATION WITH MIRRORS (74

"I was sure they'd bring it with them." — "For the sake of argument, what difference does that make? Your house is jammed to overflowing with stuff like that now." — "I even phoned them about it. Got them up out of bed." — "For the sake of argument, who cares!" — "Next time maybe I'll know better."

75) THE LATE AFTERNOON

A shadow falls across the table. . . drinks slowly of a cup, nibbles the roseleaf. . .

SUBSTANCE OF SHADOW (76

And when a thousand years have passed. . . Ah. Ah, yes. Shadowy figures of the little earth. . . Appointments which will not wait, which must be kept. Ah. Ah, yes. The worm at the heart of the roseleaf.

77) THE HEART'S UNDERSTANDING

Above all I wish you joy in the things which are fashioned for joy, and an honest sorrow in what is of its nature sorrowful. Joy and sorrow — each is beautiful, and beautiful the heart's understanding of them.

THE BALANCE SHEET (78

Of all things save the doings of the heart, of a generous, unpossessing, free heart, ample to its own inclinations and needless of every other, when a life is at an end, O, of all things save this alone, what remains? What remains save those moments when heart wept, or when it burst in gladness. . ?

79) DUST'S ONLY ENEMY

A good and gentle heart. . . In this world there is nothing more beautiful.

WONDER REMAINS WONDER (80

There is in each life a quality, a special fragrance of the bone and of the flesh, individual, unmistakeable, exactly as it issued from the spirit's mold. A quality which nothing can in any manner alter.

85) A DIFFICULT UNDERTAKING

This day of life, to render some unimportantness beautiful. Without "effort," "thought," or "cunning," to do that; and to leave it — whether "gesture," "look," or "touching" — intact and untarnished in its ordained place. What an undertaking!

NONESSENTIALISM IN PRACTICE (86

It's nonessential: 7) to recognize the inescapable poignancy of the world, and all that takes place in it; one has only to make "a brave effort" to discover "one's own true, *personal* set of 'values' " — through an "objective and sound, unflinching appraisal of 'things as they *really* are.' " This should do the trick very nicely.

87) THE FARAWAY BALLAD

Soulless; cold are the fishes that sleep in the grove. Soulless; cold the fishes!

THE WORST SIN (88

Tonight, so quietly. . . *To offer something which the heart has colored and made its own.* I am constantly amazed at how arrogant people are; in the wonders and mysteries of this world, not to be humble!

81) MORE FABULOUS ANIMALS

This one may best be described as a "translation" — sort of a "brought-over." Think of a hallway made of wish-sponges, of a fruit tasting of street-cries: put them together, gingerly, tenderly — "add" *memories*. . .

THE LITTLE ESSAYS (82

Is Tomorrow Here? Of course. Tomorrow was a cooked goose from the moment it commenced to flash back a few of its least appetizing skills. Everyone saw them as "Progress" — Yes, chucking tomorrow's kitbag into the soup before anybody got round to caring what kind of soup would be a sensible soup to have.

83) CONVERSATION WITH MIRRORS

"For the sake of argument, suppose a revelation." — "Define your terms." — "From despair alone. . . "

NONESSENTIALISM IN PRACTICE (84

It's nonessential: 1) to believe; 2) to believe in believing; 3) to believe in believing in believing; 4) to believe in not believing; 5) to believe in not believing in believing; 6) to believe in not believing in believing in not believing.

89) GLAD ABOUT ANIMALS

I am glad about animals, about their many different kinds and appearances. I find it a pleasure to look at them, wonder about them, to wonder what they wonder about me. Wonderful comicals of their kind; of mine.

GLAD ABOUT FISHES&BIRDS (90

I am glad about the eagerplacid way they accept the miracle of themselves. It's marvelous the way they manneroffactly set about the business of gathering horsetailhairs for their nests and zoom-diving up over waterfalls and all the rest of it. Angels haven't it half over them! *What respect they have for their own methods.*

91) GLAD ABOUT SNAKES&SCORPIONS

I am glad about all the crawling things; their strange — and ever grace-filled — dignities.

GLAD ABOUT SEA&SKY (92

I am glad about this ever-changing and ever-renewing marriage — which seems to be celebrated more out of this world than in it. Glad of that watching blueness — which always disconcerts the more it reassures.

93) THE MODERN SICKNESS

On every hand there is a nasty slyness, a petty viciousness; not to serve any purpose really, just out of sheer inner spite — a nasty, vicious slyness. A nothing-for-nothing affair; petty, nasty, vicious — a sort of vegetarian cannibalism.

AN "HONEST" POLITICIAN (94

Himself he hired to speak at a dinner in his honor. All went well except anybody else could have hoked up something to say for him: he could think of nothing. "This unregenerate heel" is how he started; then he lapsed into censure of the most telling kind; and concluded, "But now, all flattery aside — "

95) BEWARE THE HARVEST

A petty, nasty, for-the-hell-of-it slyness is deliberately fashioned forth as "the modern mode." Look about you!

CONVERSATION WITH MIRRORS (96

"You. . . you make no effort to appreciate another point of view. You. . . errr. . . " — "How odd that you find your own tolerable. I find it detestable." — "You. . . you won't— just *willfully* won't see that. . . that. . . errr . . . " — "Oh, come now."

97) PORTRAITS ON WATER

Behold, then, this Old Grandfather Thing. A sneering, tired dull-green coat; high collar like an albino wolf's lips; the face shadowed over with little filths of petulant selfishnesses; in sum, a worthless, dirty, grayly decaying baby. Ah, flow swiftly. . .

SCENES OF CHILDHOOD (98

The air is striped like a circus tent; yellow, red, green. A great horse with golden mane is nubbling the tops of barns and steeples. Lovely in the tall grass. . . lying breathless and naked under the hot tent. . . Blowing locks of bushes, king's robe-crimson jewels flashing in the warm, silken spray. . . O caressing hands of the goddess. . ! !

99) I AM THE

Golden Browed Lion of the Waters. Come! *my gentle curls, sir; my cruelkind hands, m'lady.*

OTELLME'S AND WHEREDO'S (100

O tell me how I may clean my heart for the touching of such loveliness! Where do the cold gems sparkling there in the soft, purple curls of the meadow go to be reset and polished?

101) OTELLME'S AND WHEREDO'S

O tell me when the small lips of birds are at their bitter weeping in the wood, how shall I find tongue for the sorrow that's in me? Where do the sweet powers of the hushed heart gather?

I AM THE (102

King Who Disdains All Kingdoms, greater than the rending frost at the heart of a winter tree, less than the foam on the sea-bird's wing. I am the King Who Consumes All Kingdoms, mightier than the sea's voice under a north wind, far more affrighted than the break-breath prayer of a man dying.

103) SCENES OF CHILDHOOD

The hands of the old horse are picking withered, tired steps off the road.

PORTRAITS ON WATER (104

Behold, then, the Faithful One. Her breasts are wrinkled and shrunken now, like lumps of charred dough. Years, years of a life, they are there on her face as clawmarks; the beast has been at her — she is burnt dry under him. The sacred writing, the writing that tells of life's closing age. . . and of death's opening youth.

105) SCENES OF CHILDHOOD

They gave us many little princesses to play with. Often three or four a day. And all of them enchanted. We did all sorts of jolly-dance things to wake them up. But they'd go away. Damn.

PORTRAITS ON WATER (106

Behold, then, the Sleeping Child. Arms folded around a glass-box which holds all the capital D's in the world. They shimmer and dance in the moonlight. One of them comes to rest on her mouth; another on her throat. . . Now the ugliest D of all — dark, dark. . . like a toaddog — it squats watching on her innocent forehead. . . watching all the others go away.

107) OTELLME'S AND WHEREDO'S

O tell me of the Hill of Waking Sleep! Where do the silent sing. . . ?

I AM THE (108

Long Cold House of Unending Sleep. Pale stainless hounds stand eternal guard that no errant sound or unwanted incitement mar the slumber of my guests. Plan to stay the night here; its peace is quite contagious.

109) I AM THE

Joy of the Desiring Flesh. The days of my living are summer days; the nights of my glory outshine the blazing wave-caps of the heavens at their floodtide! Mine is the confident hand shaping this world.

OTELLME'S AND WHEREDO'S (110

O tell me have you ever rounded the little curve-end of the land where the hills are like lovers parting in the woeful fret and press of the surf as it thunders upon the rocks with their graybrown toes like a giant's. . . and it and them as children crying for boats lost on a pond? Where do the severed of living go for their healing. . . ?

111) PORTRAITS ON WATER

Behold, then, the Ancient Queen. Summer cringes at her fingers' ends. . . their wiltingcold spreading everywhere.

SCENES OF CHILDHOOD (112

Prudence drank of the moonhoney spilling upon the lawn; Caution got smashed under the tread of an appleblossom; Manly Reserve was carried off on the saddle of a junebug; Proper Respect for Elders succumbed in the process of a becoming that was more like a begoing. But bless them and me.

113) KINDNESS OF CLOWNS

But if houses are many things to many people, they can be even fewer things to fewer people. And clowns, being always fewer — because nicer — than anybody, a house less than one to them becomes "*FORALL*."

MY JOURNEY'S JOURNEYING (114

Might I have been your Inn beyond this brief night-place's stopping — O spirit, poor guest, sinking down at the woodsedge in this great dark where all lives are hidden. Might I have been a voice speaking back from the realm of what has not yet been, I would have told you not to come!

115) KINDNESS OF CLOWNS

Suspicion made the first pairapants; but, Joey, it'll be love'll take off the last.

CONVERSATION WITH MIRRORS (116

"Why do you suppose they keep moving the candles from one window to the other?" — "To show that there's something doing inside there." — "Something doing?" — "Yes, something doing. Like showing you where the dark is sparklingest!"

117) GOLDEN PLUM BUDS

We imagine one another so badly. We confuse one another with appearances that form in chairs and oceanliners and with being some longago-Greek or "young girl walking across field at sevenpm April3rd" or being "mykeeper'sbrother."

GOLDEN PLUM BUDS (118

Whatever we imagine for one another is wrong to the extent that we separate a state of being from its doesness. Because all appearances have a common origin in the unseeable fluidity *which issues forth from the action of its own flowing*. Existence is verb. (No "objects," no "things-to-be-named"— *doing itself does itself do*.)

119) MY INNOCENT COMPANIONS

They imagine an earth, a sky; imagine that they are alive: and they die.

FRIEND THE RABBIT (120

He imagines himself a bird with long ears, ball-y tail, chassis lovingly covered with soft golden fur. At sea a fortnight he sights a ship, but everybody a-bored pretends to see only a flying rabbit.

121) MORE FABULOUS ANIMALS

The "being a twig in a child's hand" animal has intent and lovely eyes. (Do you, even now, O rose-hued silhouette, imagine a moment when life can permit its gaze to wander from the "unseen"?)

WHERE IS EVERYONE? (122

If you say pardon it won't matter. If you say sorry-sorry it won't get you covered with no godhair. If you say I am a nicer place than where I am it won't get you overlapped with the Princess of the Submerged Pyramid. But if you say beautifulbeautifulmoon they'll lower the boom!

123) MORE FABULOUS ANIMALS

The "being something distant and striding" animal won't bequeath you any Gospels For Gallowsbait.

WHERE IS EVERYONE? (124

If you say nodice it won't genuinate. If you say gitoutaherejack it won't do them no droop. If you say I don't fit me nomore it won't splug. But if you say hurrahhurraheverybody then watch out!

125) A NIGHT SONG

You letter makes me think of two eyes, very beautiful, very thoughtful, but somehow. . . *only* eyes — I mean there's no face to go with them! Oh, it's not what you think — nothing *that* simple. No matter.

VISIT AMONG TREES (126

So that's why I have come here: some part of me has demanded that I come. That's why I may not explain it now — at least until I am less clear about it. Other parts of me are waiting in other un-damaged places — waiting to be sorted, assembled, identified: they will tell me when.

127) VISIT AMONG TREES

Garden us in this loneliness of outer selves — O eyes of what we see!

A NIGHT SONG (128

I am not interested in any of that: you may believe what you like. The detail of the whole, there's all and enough generality to last me a while. Begging the issue? Yep, on my knees!

129) A NIGHT SONG

No, it's not just to be another make-damn funny onion with legs, piddling up his little puddle of "opinions" and "moral convictions" so that some even worse fool may be tempted over for a sniff. . .

A NIGHT SONG (130

I am glad you like the other version, but suspect someone of priming your lag in the matter of those "tied boxes." You do have your hushed side: not to be spooky about it, all compliments are troubling — when they're not just longgeorged tiresome. Of course everyone is serious; that's what's so dam BSquarish!

131) A NIGHT SONG

And flies *also* are thicker than water. "Overtones of psychopathological intensity." — "Pa-llease! not *that* chickenchat!"

THE POLEMIST'S COW (132

Avec are clover 'n butterclups this other one, a Dog that up to me in unambiguous haste arrives; who am I? some private-gabbed Pericles warming his rostrum with ept albeit provincial supplications? — Friar Middenstomp, open that beer!

133) THE ONLY DOG

Which was a Cat soon found that to follow the fashion of his kind he must leg it round the rascals while yet the Sun and the Moon and the Pretty Dandelion were in respectful accord.

THE ONLY DEARLITTLEOWL (134

Which was an Allblack Polar Bear fell down some water. O what's the worry, he could still be pinning them up. He could still be running the ole horn in under the wallpaper. So! in full stride! away and alas, for Jesus and the little dimpled angels whose bags are all safely checked 'n counted.

135) WHERE IS EVERYONE?

If you say Godnods they won't bootyer. But if you say damnoodlewits oh brother!

THE ONLY GREATLION (136

Which was a Parttime Clock began to cling outside a little because you will be well and you will be wondered O when on some other star all those second thoughts have time to get thunk.

137) ANOTHER DAY GONE

This. . . and it is already that. On, on we go, baffled by the shadow of this In-Out; baffled to that point of cunning which declares: It is so little, it is nothing, it is enough.

NONESSENTIALISM IN PRACTICE (138

It's nonessential to believe that the special quality of every life resides not in its being (if by being we mean being *somewhere:* and if we don't, whose else's tail shall we chase?), but in its strange motionability, its headlong flight from anything and everything that even remotely smacks of "this day", "this place".

139) NONESSENTIALISM IN PRACTICE

It's nonessential to reject all "dayness"; thought is of what "is". — (But *where's* "thought"?)

KINDNESS OF CLOWNS (140

So all was a day! We planted the rosebush as a sign of peace between our leagues. Cheer up, lad; your arguments sound like do but smell like don't — so, let's spit us some fatter hares.

141) THE LITTLE ESSAYS

What Is Right? Much depends on whether you want to grow nettles or clover: on whether you've come to applaud or just to swipe clothes off the line; on whether you bring a halter or a head-dress.

THE ONLY HEN (142

Which was a Butterfly had to cross the ocean five times before she could get a shirtwaist that halfway suited; and even then she didn't think the back quite bonny enough — so she put it in front and sat on it until everybody had gone home. Then she fetched out a bottle and got skyeyed.

143) FRIEND THE RABBIT

He came dancing in and presented her with a child asleep on a leaf.

I AM THE (144

One Who Sits Watching You. Without feeling that there is too much at stake; without feeling that it really matters very much what becomes of you. — What goes on inside that leaf is more important anyway.

145) BRIGHT *OMBRES CHINOIS*

Because something here does not enchant, are those little stars,
so brilliant! so abiding! to be accounted faults of a like unlording
. . . the Tale allow no child ever again to say, "Look! whose
eyes are those?"

ALL ARE ANIMALS (146

You know that trees are animals like any others; just as flowers
and lakes — and even what we think and what we say, what
we dream, what we imagine — these too are animals, animals
like any others. And stars, and sky, the moon, the sun, the earth
— oh, yes, these too! all are animals!

147) BRIGHT *OMBRES CHINOIS*

The animal of sleep — ah, within this one we pass our
lives; until suddenly. . . !

POOR PUCCIO D'ANIELLO (148

Oh, come along, admit it! On Monday we shall! what, on Tues-
day we shall not, on Wednesday we shall rot — which leaves
the rest of the week for counting blessings. Ah, we are the fort-
unate vegetables!

149) FLIES HAVE FINGERS

With which they hold their food. Just as any paulr duke phutzing around the carbarn in hopes of making an impression on the motorman's daughter, who sometimes at late afternoon has been known to peek in.

FLIES HAVE FINGERS (150

"Ah, dear maryanne lowder, howdydo, howdydo, gel; my heart it is napoleon-shaped — why, even my ears and teeth they be like that bloody elf's!" But it's only a machinist back to check over the switchbox into which some small boys yesterday jammed a riflebutt. "Howdydo, yerself! n'stop gnawin on thet gawddum wheel!"

151) FLIES HAVE FINGERS

With which they don't sign treaties. Or write speeches. Or applaud ulyssesqnuisances.

FLIES HAVE FINGERS (152

And the feet of the air, toes; but what is maryanne lowder doing off in yonder ballpark with jackb handy, the oily machinist? — And out of all the all. . . apes'n meadowlarks, meat, bread, cornlikker'n anewmoon!

153) COMMENTS FOR STRINGEDHORNS

You say, Let them have it, and I don't know whether you mean, Let them have it, or, Let them have it; whether you hanker to join or disjoint these intellectual pimps, liberal punks, and college-poetiquettes.

COMMENTS FOR STRINGEDHORNS (154

I once thought that if people got a good whiff of what is really with all these lying, swindling, sanctimonious Democracy-pushers, they'd make some kind of instinctive grab for the flush; but I'masonofagun! it's worth your neck keeping out of their way as they come charging hellbent right up to the bowl's edge!

155) A NIGHT SONG

Your letter must have pleased you to write: it's so beautifully, so *seriously* petty.

A NIGHT SONG (156

No, I don't care to go on with the "Comments." Let the swine have their green-frothed swill. Shlup! Shlup! Only let them hurry it. Meantime, — oh, I almost forgot to thank you for the books!

POEM XL SCAPE

157) APRIL 6, 1956

The day begins in the morning. You get your pants and shirt on, open the door, a man says, "OK, just pay me half now, you'll get the rest of your horse later; here's the bridle."

APRIL 6, 1956 (158

Around Noon the afternoon begins. You put the franks'n friedbeans on the plate, man walks in leading a green duck on a string. "Your horse likes the company of a duck, but your only charge is for the gold chain." — "What gold chain?" — "The one your duck swallowed. D'you think they come that color!"

159) APRIL 6, 1956

(O little duck, why d'you keep edging up to that damn telephone? It's disconnected.)

APRIL 6, 1956 (160

Sundown... You set bottles'n glasses out, man walks in with two long goofy paper ears stuck to his hatband, does a pile on the floor, says, "You weren't expecting a *real* horse for that price, were you?"

161) THIS BEWILDERING HOUSE

All of us are at the window, looking out of this strange room; men. . . whose skins on one side are black, are yellow, are brown, are white, are red — standing close together in this bewildering house.

WHAT FANTASTIC CREATURES! (162

I look out of this window — that is what it is like there, for all who look out of windows, from apartments, from farmhouses, from churches, jails, schoolrooms, cityhalls: the sky and a street, fields, bridges, waterfalls. . . my God! these are all such *strange* things! and those "people" moving there, what extraordinarily fantastic creatures!

163) BARNS, SALOONS, BROTHELS

Who'd care for a glimpse of these things *turned to flesh*. . . and staring back!

IN MOMENTARY ETERNITY (164

O bluebell my brother! Tiger! sparrow! moon! and snowflake too! O great brothers! One little one of us looks out of me—but O how many, many of me are looking out of you, dear brothers!

165) WITH THIS ROSE

I thee wake. And in this room — yes, to become preoccupied with . . . oh, I don't know, let's say, God's digestion, one must be convinced that nearer matters aren't worth too much: *responsibilities, mysteries, devotions, are here.*

ALGO Ó NADA (166

Truth must in. We are the work. The made-world is all decoration, and only matters that when it is not completely given over to its appointed task of providing a setting of the most consummate brutality, sterility, and hideousness, it is just plain ridiculously *silly!* Look about you — those clothes, houses, cars — woweee!!

167) YOU'RE ALL NUTS

Boobs, scamps, frauds, and all you assorted blaugh-swilling drearies — oh, COME OFF IT!

SUNDAY, APRIL 8th (168

With this rose I thee world. Fashioned in Love, its color the color of heart'sblood! See, though its leaves do wilt and fall, yet is it rose; and never any mean or sullied thing. Wonder it!

A Letter to God

A Letter to God

the wing is burning wing is burning O burn the wing for the
wing is burning

My heart is not in the things here.

Men have made no effort to live by your word or by the word of
any Good. This has angered me always. Childhood had not the color
of the beautiful but of poverty and learning to kill what was best to
know and love or be. So I write out of an awkward shyness; not
understanding the angel. And the way to be near you I understand
not. And the methods of love and joy and light are not understood.
Nor of hate and pain and fear is there any manner or need not known.

This black village. Houses, a lake and . . . *(eye of fire O the Eye
is on fire)* gray loose frog
squatting on the arms of the Cross

I first went to school in a town of steel. The boys had faces like
thin cats—the geography of evil; the history of monsters—I want to
remind you that I understand little in your sense. Sometimes I pick
up a stone in the street, and just hold it in my hand. That may have
nothing to do with present difficulties in the world; but it gives me
pleasure and can cause no ultimate harm to anyone. I was fifteen
before I got all of myself in. Until then I seemed to smile when I felt
angry, grit my teeth together when expected to talk. My clothes never
pleased me in color or in the way they felt when I took them off at

45

night. They were like the skin of an animal I knew nothing about. The same with my teeth: often they were cold and felt too sharp in my mouth.

    1915: Yellow snow in Cleveland. Lame woman swinging a rope.

    1922: To kill of course: "Don't stare at me!"

    1923: And the flesh was made a ward.

    1928: Her crying made me cry. Moved to new hungers. Like nosebleed.

    1931: And the Church . . . glittering throats in a gray choir.

    1934: It is not always easy to live a good life.

Water is cruel water is cold kind water deep sweet water O then let me be quiet and quiet and still. For stranger stronger art thou.

    "Do you hate me?"

    "I know thee not—not even in fear."

Black tree . . . rust run house of darkness lake of evil
           cabin terrible wren spool grin MILK leaf light
scrubwoman dip your mop in the skittering pail of heaven
merchant sell on the playful blood of untroubling boys, *you snake!*
king put your sword to the land of light and land the great fish
You God tame
O make tame what men call war
but is the only condition of their 'peace'

    O loud sing the leaving lark

Yesterday I tried to remember the first time I ever tasted an apple. Then I thought of this letter to you and it seemed an unimportant thing to know. . .

But I'm not sure.

Certainly your patterns are bigger than mine. And . . .

Why don't you come down and carry on your fight? What exactly did you mean when you said

"Thou shalt not kill."?

Come down God and continue your fight against this pious murder. —"Under certain circumstances; in order to properly defend; in event that no other method of survival is forthcoming"—

NO

"Thou shalt not kill."

And what right has anyone to make people think you were a liar.

My father used to say that I looked too long at people. It is true that they suspected me of not understanding them, and this made them want to make me uneasy; which they did by gripping my shoulder or by turning suddenly away.

November 16, 1939: I am first conscious of another being in myself.

Banners

hoofs (O the swift graceful target)

a wound perhaps

I question not your authority.

Nor my own.

I make preparation to use them.

Has lived. Loves. In the world!

Just as there is no end to joy in life . . . an existence resembling every beautiful. Cry not. Be not mean. Do not cheat. Make no money out of blood. Believe in man. Belief in man is God.

the use of guilt is death

People look out of the holes in their eyes.
The eye itself is of the spirit.
Not to see, but seeing.

O an inch from the rosebush or a thousand miles from this
murder . . . this being here!
Ghost, ghost upon the sea, have you tidings?
have you angels found?
O a tiny place away from the world where we may lie,
my love and me?
            Blockhead!
Dear God, I don't want to go to bed tonight. There should be a
lock on what I have to think.

December 5, 1939: Visited by a man and woman from another
world.
December 7, 1939: Wilbur (you would like him) broke a piece
out of a poem by One of the Lads (can never tell them apart) and
used it as the headstone for a gnat he had got fond of.
December 8, 1939: Spent the day filing a complaint against the
U.S. Senate. Rather pleased to know I have a say in matters per-
taining to.
December 9, 1939: Walked down Cornelia Street. Met nobody
I knew nor did anyone else.
December 14, 1942: Planning a little surprise for my enemies.
More about this anon, I reckon.

August 13, 1943: Wilbur and I discussed the policy of Our State Dept. To be sure. And How. You said it.

I have no children because I couldn't feed them. My wife never has a new coat and I may have to write novels. So do I do. It is a situation I wish you'd do something about because nobody else gives a damn. I can't take the rich. Means two things.

(How do you like this?)
The cave was lined with blue fur. A princess sat near the entrance, and in her hand she hald a chalice made of gold. She drank of the wine and softly died.

Far away, almost to the end of the most distant land, her lover paused at his task of creating a new being.

Two things walked through the shadow which like a woolen shawl hung on the shoulders of the air. Their faces were streaked with yellow chalk and a single horn grew out of their foreheads. It was night when they reached the cave.

They did not touch her. They moved to a corner away from the world, and, lowering their beautiful, sad heads, wept.

(And this?)
No one supposed the chaining of that particular beast to a tree would bring the world to an unsightly end. Nor did it. But it did effect a curious condition in the lives of three people who had their home a score of miles out at sea.

It was the howling.

It was a sense on the air that terror had a face which could be seen. And feet really which walked in search of open graves.

The three were John Jefferson.

They had been so named by a wave which took them to mother.
One was tall with box-deep eyes. One was fair, slim-skulled and
strong as thrice-heated tea. The third was almost a Christ—he. . .
O John Jefferson!
What will become of thee?
O what, what will become of thee?

To be whole!
—how we hunger to be clean!
—these dazzling messengers from white suns—
Is it possible to
You smile, God

November 16, 1941: "It's going to snow soon," I said.
I ruffled her hair as she set the table. She crumpled back the
bread-wrapper and cut five slices. I pulled up the chairs. The cat
rubbed against my legs as we sat down. Suddenly we both laughed
and I got up and went around to kiss her. She pushed me away
and made a crinkly face. "Eat, you big silly," she said; but she
sprang to her feet and pressed her body hard against mine. Holding
her in my arms with a savage joy, I glanced out of the window:
"Ah Christ! will you just look at it snow," I said.

They moved into the circle
which a snail had drawn
on the forehead of a weeping lion

This marble casket. *O laughing maiden . . .*
war perhaps. Be not unwary, God. The war
draws no circle
. . . .
Killed in action,
Sept. 24, 1945

You know as well as I do
that . . .

It is without doubt unfortunate that the truly beautiful part was
destroyed before anyone could see it. I know I would now like much
to have even the dimmest knowledge of its perfections.

Whatever your hidden motives were, there does seem to have
been shown a tragic carelessness in the manner of the defilement.
Something else surely could have been done with us—even at the
final moment—even in the white hour of your agony when you
regretted your lowly creation, might not some smallest vestige of
mercy have been spared . . ?

I am not able to say how exactly it would have altered my
holdings, but I am not far off believing a dog might better have been
commissioned to the endeavors I have before me.

I think of the girl I loved when I was twelve. I think of the
thousands of eyes and voices that have gone through her since then.
Perhaps she is dead. . .

I think of the creek I used to walk along coming from school.
Of the teacher who shot himself in front of the solid geometry class.
Of the time I said a lively Anglo-Saxon word by mistake in assem-
bly. . .

I think of my father being carried home with half his foot cut off in the mill. I think of my brother driving around town in a low-slung, tan racing car he picked up in a junkyard for sixteen bucks. Of my uncle stumbling into High Mass drunk as a lord and undressing at the altar. . . .

What are you thinking of at this moment, God?

I cannot really expect the old man to take his feet out of the river and make a saddle for a horse nobody would want to ride anyway.

He looks up and winks at me as I go tearing by with some plan or other to stop everybody from running straight on to hell.

Perhaps he understands in the way he has always understood the things which at all concern him.

But it never seriously appeals to him to take his feet out of the gently flowing water.

May 27, 1942: I have seen the new being.

Aside to your daughter Keela:

I am not permitted to speak to you when the white leopard is in the room. On the evening of Peretho (Jan. 6 in heaven) you will walk under the lemon trees which your father planted. You will wear the pink dress with the margarineflies on the collar. Do not grow bitter if I do not always accompany you to market. The eyes of the geese in their paper crates look with too much pity upon us. Perhaps the wan leopard will not come today . . . say, how is this? The blood will have dried on his paws by the time our true representation to the Other One can be made—

May 28, 1942: The light is blinding.

In runaway order

out of the green life

O ALL IN FIRE

mother

Some useless fellow. My cold rule, on nineth hill. . .
every murder is the murder of Thee

as I everliving lean in love up to that bright tree

Silence then!
"This day is death's."
Red full sweet beast.   .

"What time is it in the tiger's garden?"
You damned cheats eating your kill—
Bloody handed pigs
Defying Thy announced will
It is hard to have friends now. People are going to pieces too
fast. They hate anyone who does not bleed fog and sickness.
I watch the young men go. Nothing can heal them.
Death won't. These are machine-made . . . not meant to feel or
to think—
What have you told them, God, that they go thus to slay and to
be slain—
WHAT HAS ANYONE TOLD THEM?

May 29, 1942: All I am ever kind to—
    "Wear the shawl His mother made."
    "I've given it away."
    "Given it away . . ?"
    "Yes—To the one of evil."

Then for the good!

Blackness in the mouth of their walking. Is it profitable to be
merciful ... Joy, moon, *moon*—"Long ago the world rode away
from the village of my father."—white cold towers
   (valley of unreturning faith)
   Here they sleep.
   Who know Thee not. The bed (in blood), under low
stars
"Do not die."
Standing in their salt sweat ... hairy mouths full of a speech no man
anywhere has belief in. Big plans gone west.
These do not want Thee. Except for fun. To paint flags on Your
belly.
To make war right.

   All is a lie in their world.

   God, your noble little sons are mad.
   They breathe murder.
   Their eyes steam.
   The dimout of death.
   This day is his.
   Now is his hurry.
   More than dying, nothing is done.
   But as toads drinking snot.

   Cloud over me this cry, this togethering of a last darkness—
   I think your noble little sons are
thieves and cutthroats
stewing in their mess   Go low Light.
fouling the pants of an idiot   Build a throne.

STAR

And the horizon of love was the morning of the 8th day.

Ah, the hogwild jades of murder neigh. . .

I order you to destroy them.
I am tired of their dirt.
We have a right to live!
None shall kill when all are comforted.
Give us the earth now.
Give us the peace now.
Give us the daily bread now.
O give us the land and the creatures of the field and the silent
beautiful wood
    that we may feed and shelter
    all men equally
    for man's only duty is to man.

God, we shall accept the terms of your world.
That we may not kill.
That we may not hate.
That the things of labor belong to all men.
That the things of spirit live in all men.
That the things of God are on earth for the use of all men.

None shall kill when all are completed.
None shall hate when all are at love.

                                        August, 1943.